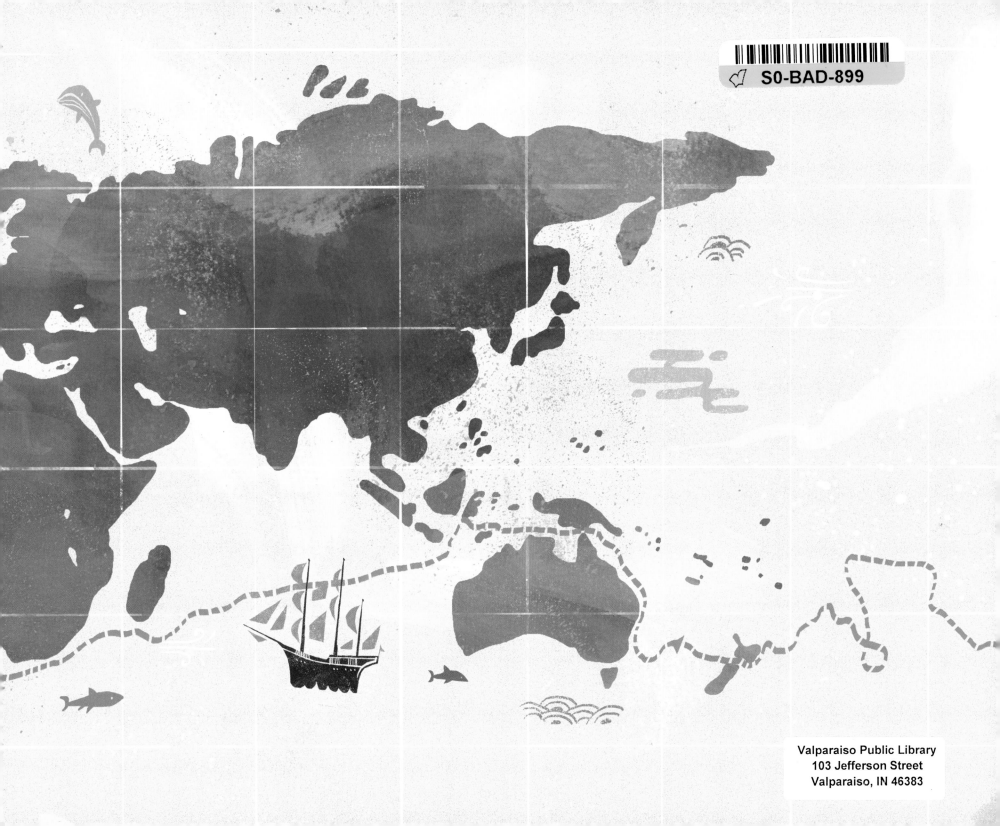

Also in the *Meet*... series

And look out for more great *Meet*... books coming soon

Meet... CAPTAIN COOK

WRITTEN BY RAE MURDIE
ILLUSTRATED BY CHRIS NIXON

RANDOM HOUSE AUSTRALIA

For my motley crew – the Gipps family. RM

For my beautiful fiancée, Lisa, and those brave enough to explore. CN

A Random House book
Published by Random House Australia Pty Ltd
Level 3, 100 Pacific Highway, North Sydney NSW 2060
www.randomhouse.com.au

First published by Random House Australia in 2013

Text © Random House Australia 2013
Illustrations © Chris Nixon 2013

The moral right of the author and the illustrator has been asserted.

Addresses for companies within the Random House Group can be found at
www.randomhouse.com.au/offices

National Library of Australia
Cataloguing-in-Publication Entry

Author: Murdie, Rae
Title: Meet Captain Cook / Rae Murdie; Chris Nixon, illustrator
ISBN: 978 0 85798 017 5 (hbk.)
Series: Meet; 3.
Target Audience: For children.
Subjects: Cook, James, 1728–1779
Explorers – Great Britain – Juvenile literature.
Discoveries in geography – English – Juvenile literature.
Voyages around the world – Juvenile literature.
Pacific Area – Discovery and exploration – Juvenile literature.
Other Authors/Contributors: Nixon, Chris, illustrator
Dewey Number: 910.92

Cover and internal illustrations © Chris Nixon
Cover design by Kirby Armstrong
Internal design by Christabella Designs
Printed and bound in China by Midas Printing

Captain James Cook was an English explorer in the British Royal Navy.

In 1768 Captain Cook and his crew on the HMB *Endeavour* set sail from England in search of new lands and scientific knowledge.

This is the story of how Captain Cook discovered the east coast of New Holland (Australia) on that voyage.

Before Captain James Cook became a famous explorer, he was . . .

a baby born in a
two-room cottage

a schoolboy

a farm boy

a worker in a seaside store

a sailor's apprentice
studying at night

a husband, a father,

and a mariner in
Britain's Royal Navy.

In the Navy James Cook studied astronomy, science and maths, all the while dreaming of one day commanding his own ship on epic voyages.

He lived in a time of great exploration and scientific discovery. Nations raced to unlock the secrets of the world and its oceans.

So when James was asked to lead an expedition for England, he accepted with pride. He was to captain a ship bound for King George's Island. From there he was to chart the transit of the planet Venus across the sun.

Captain Cook was also handed a sealed letter from the King. He was given firm instructions to open it only when this mission was complete.

Captain Cook set about preparing for the expedition.

For weeks he studied ...

... and planned ...

... and calculated.

Of all the boats in England, a coal ship was chosen for the voyage. Though small, the ship was **sturdy** and **strong**. She was refitted and christened the HMB *Endeavour.*

In August 1768, the *Endeavour* embarked on her maiden voyage with great pomp and fanfare. Among those onboard were a variety of animals, 55 sailors, a one-handed cook, an astronomer, four artists and a botanist by the name of Joseph Banks.

This motley crew readied themselves for the dangers of the open seas and the strange lands that were rumoured to lie ahead.

The *Endeavour* made her way down the coast of Africa in fine weather. The crew caught sharks and marvelled at flying fish. Joseph Banks spotted penguins and collected giant kelp.

But the tropics soon gave way to the violent weather of the South Atlantic. Captain Cook and his crew prepared for the challenge of rounding Cape Horn. After three failed attempts, the *Endeavour* overcame icy winds and bitter gales to forge through the dreaded passage and emerge into the South Pacific.

After eight long months at sea, the crew dropped anchor off the coast of King George's Island. The locals paddled out to welcome them. They traded fresh food in exchange for beads and metal tools.

Captain Cook and his men built a fort and an observatory, where on a clear day they gathered to watch Venus pass across the sun.

At last it was time to open the King's secret letter.
It revealed a new and most important task:
to venture south in search of new land.

The Dutch had already discovered New Zealand and parts of
the neighbouring continent of New Holland. But both were still
unmapped. And there were whispers that the Pacific Ocean
was also home to a great southern land, *Terra Australis*.

Captain Cook was to find it and claim it for the King.

Captain Cook sailed the *Endeavour* southwards without a map.
He steered by the sun and the stars over seas as wide as the sky. When
no new land was found, the *Endeavour* turned west, passing whales
and seals and albatross.

Supplies onboard ran low, and without land in sight, the crew grew tired and homesick.

When at last Captain Cook spotted seaweed and driftwood with barnacles, he was sure New Zealand was near.

At New Zealand's
Poverty Bay, Captain Cook and his
crew faced fierce Maori warriors.
Once an understanding was
reached, the crew bartered
for fish, lobster and even stingray.

  With fresh supplies onboard,
Captain Cook set about exploring New
Zealand's inlets and bays. He surveyed its
islands and completed his circumnavigation
of the country in just six months.

Captain Cook then turned his sights towards New Holland. Again the *Endeavour* and her crew headed out to sea.

They voyaged northwest until early one morning the sloping hills of southeastern New Holland came into view. It was a sight no European had seen before.

But foul winds kept the *Endeavour* at sea. For days, Captain Cook and his crew sailed up the coast. They spotted smoke in the sky and saw men and women of dark skin living on the land.

When the gales eased and the sea calmed, the *Endeavour* weighed
anchor in a sheltered bay and her weary crew made dry land.

The locals seemed to want them gone, but the Englishmen persisted

The crew barrelled fresh water and caught more fish than all hands could eat.

Joseph Banks ventured inland. He observed strange animals, collected flora, and examined the soils and waterways.

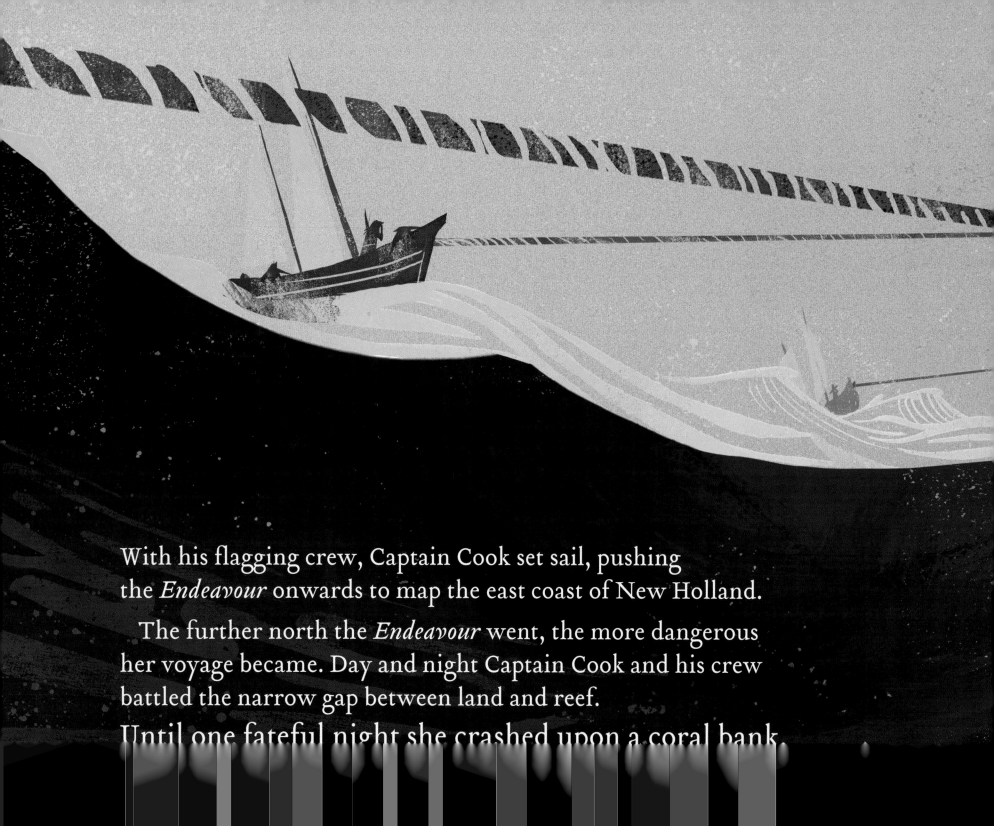

With his flagging crew, Captain Cook set sail, pushing
the *Endeavour* onwards to map the east coast of New Holland.

   The further north the *Endeavour* went, the more dangerous
her voyage became. Day and night Captain Cook and his crew
battled the narrow gap between land and reef.
Until one fateful night she crashed upon a coral bank.

Captain Cook commanded his men to heave. But the ship wouldn't budge and water came rushing in.

At high tide, Captain Cook again rallied his crew.
Exhausted, the men heaved and heaved then heaved again . . .

At last the *Endeavour* came free, but she was still leaking and in urgent need of repair.

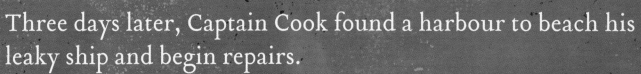

Three days later, Captain Cook found a harbour to beach his leaky ship and begin repairs.

The crew caught turtles and picked wild greens. They saw straw-coloured *wolves*, fat *alligators* and a strange-looking beast with a long tail and a hop like a rabbit.

An uneasy truce was struck with the locals. Fish were exchanged and new language was learned, including the word for the strange-looking beast.

After several weeks the *Endeavour* was ready to set sail with the first fair wind.

Captain Cook surveyed the land and its waters. From the very tip of the continent, he plotted a course to navigate the *Endeavour* clear of danger and out to open sea.

On behalf of England and King George III, Captain Cook claimed the east coast and called it New South Wales.

It was now time to return home.

Was New Holland the great *Terra Australis*?
Or did the Pacific Ocean hold more undiscovered continents?
Captain Cook did not know, but he vowed to one day return and find out.

TIMELINE

1725 (10 October): James Cook's parents, James Cook senior, a Scottish farm labourer, and Grace Pace, marry.

1728 (27 October): James Cook is born in the village of Marton-in-Cleveland in Yorkshire, England. He is the second of eight children.

1736: The Cook family moves to the village of Great Ayton, where James senior works as a farm manager for the local landowner, Thomas Skottowe. Their benefactor takes an interest in young James and pays for his schooling.

1745: At age 17, James takes a job at a local grocery store and haberdashery in the fishing village of Staithes.

1746: James is apprenticed to Whitby shipowner, John Walker, with hopes of learning the life of a merchant seaman. For six years, James lives with Walker's family and devotes his evenings to navigational studies. The first ship he works on is the coal ship *Freelove*.

1750 (20 April): James becomes an Ordinary Seaman.*

1752: James is promoted to Ship's Mate and is transferred to the coal ship *Friendship*.

1755 (7 June): James joins the British Royal Navy as an Able Seaman after turning down John Walker's offer to become Master of *Friendship*. James is assigned to the *Eagle*, and in only a month is promoted to Master's Mate.

1756 (22 January): James is promoted to Boatswain, making him responsible for ropes, sails, cables, anchors, flags and boats.

1756 (18 May): England enters The Seven Years' War. During the war, James is promoted to Master and, on the *Pembroke*, plays a significant role in the British capture of Quebec.

1762 (21 December): James marries Elizabeth Batts. They will have six children, only three of whom will survive to adulthood.

1763: James is appointed King's Surveyor. His work over the next five seasons, including his mapping of the Newfoundland coast, impresses the Royal Society, Britain's leading scientific institution.

1768 (April): James accepts an offer from the Admiralty of the Royal Navy to lead an expedition to Tahiti (then called King George's Island) to chart the transit of the planet Venus across the sun. He is promoted to the rank of Lieutenant and given command of the *Endeavour*, a coal ship converted for the voyage. Three smaller boats (a longboat, a pinnace and a yawl) are specially made for the voyage, to be carried aboard the *Endeavour*.

1768 (30 July): James receives the Admiralty's instructions for the mission and is told to open a second set of instructions only when his mission in Tahiti is complete.

* James Cook held many ranks throughout his naval career. For ease of reference he is referred to as Captain James Cook throughout this story.

1768 (8 August): The *Endeavour* sets sail.

1769 (April): The expedition arrives in Matavai Bay, Tahiti, where they receive a warm welcome from the locals.

1769 (3 June): Lieutenant Cook and his fellow scientists observe the transit of Venus. The Royal Society hopes to use the information gained to calculate the distance between Earth and the sun.

1769 (July): Following the Admiralty's second set of instructions, the *Endeavour* is put to sea to begin the search for the rumoured great southern continent, *Terra Australis*. If unsuccessful, Cook is to survey New Zealand.

1769 (September) – **1770** (March): The crew of the *Endeavour* spy the eastern coast of New Zealand while searching for *Terra Australis*. Cook circumnavigates New Zealand, proving it is an island country and not the great southern continent they were looking for.

1770 (April–August): James Cook maps the east coast of Australia (then called New Holland). While travelling north along the Great Barrier Reef, the *Endeavour* is almost shipwrecked.

On 22 August, James Cook raises the British flag on Possession Island and claims the east coast of Australia for King George III. Cook then sets sail for home, doubtful that Australia is *Terra Australis*.

1771: The *Endeavour* arrives back in England on 12 July. Impressed by his account of the voyage, the Admiralty promotes James Cook to the rank of Commander.

1772–1775: James Cook is given command of the *Resolution*, and with the *Adventure*, embarks on a second voyage in search of *Terra Australis*. He tests whether a new navigational instrument, the chronometer, can keep accurate time at sea.

The expedition travels farther south than any explorer before them. They cross the Antarctic Circle twice, and Cook charts many Pacific islands, including Easter Island, Fiji and the New Hebrides. No new land is found, therefore disproving the existence of *Terra Australis*.

1775: The *Resolution* arrives in Spithead, Hampshire on 29 July. James Cook is soon after promoted to Captain.

1776 (7 March): Captain James Cook is elected a Fellow of the Royal Society.

1776–1779: Captain Cook begins an expedition, aboard the *Resolution* and alongside the *Discovery*, to search for a northwest passage between the Atlantic and the Pacific via the Arctic. He discovers Christmas Island, the Hawaiian Islands, charts the Pacific coast of North America and crosses the Arctic Circle.

1779: The expedition returns to Hawaii to carry out repairs to the ships. On 14 February Captain Cook is killed in a dispute with the Hawaiians.

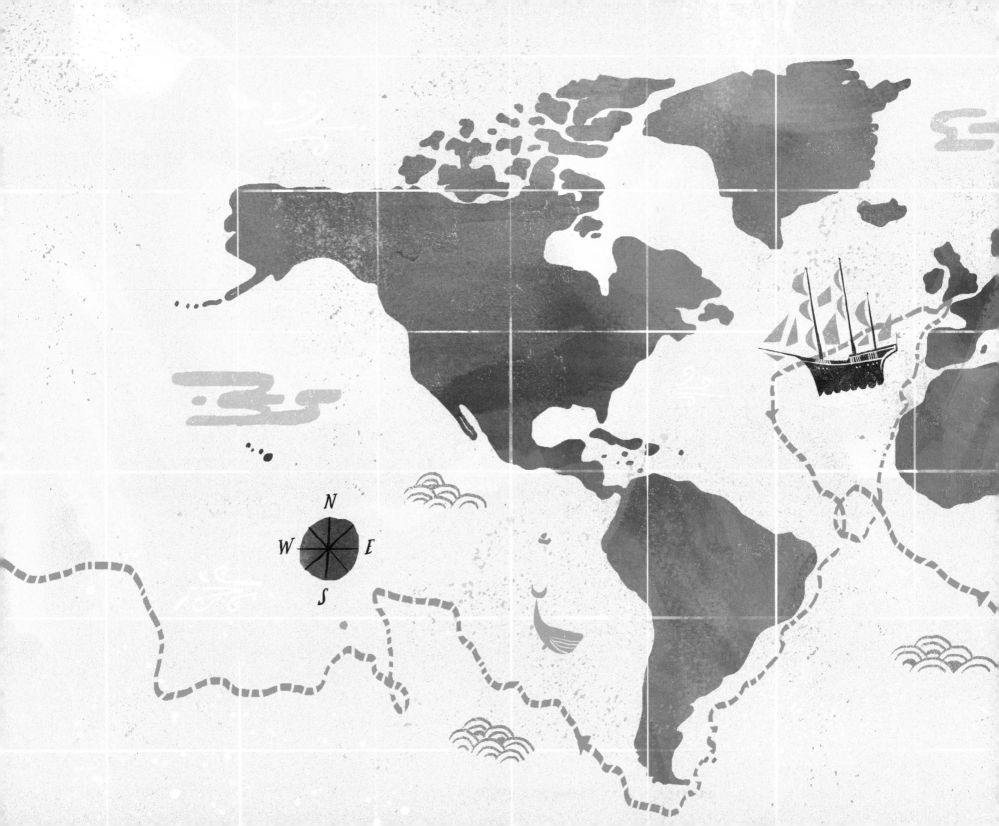